Horse

Written by Alex Hall

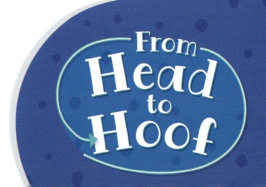

Published in 2025 by Enslow Publishing, LLC
2544 Clinton Street
Buffalo, NY 14224

© 2024 BookLife Publishing Ltd.

Written by:
Alex Hall

Edited by:
Rebecca Phillips-Bartlett

Designed by:
Jasmine Pointer

Cataloging-in-Publication Data
Names: Hall, Alex.
Title: Horse / Alex Hall.
Description: Buffalo, NY : Enslow Publishing, 2025. | Series: From head to hoof | Includes glossary.
Identifiers: ISBN 9781978541986 (pbk.) | ISBN 9781978541993 (library bound) | ISBN 9781978542006 (ebook)
Subjects: LCSH: Horses--Juvenile literature. | Horses--Anatomy--Juvenile literature. | Horses--Behavior--Juvenile literature. | Horses--Life cycles--Juvenile literature.
Classification: LCC SF302.H355 2025 | DDC 636.1--dc23

All rights reserved.

No part of this book may be reproduced in any form without permission in writing from the publisher, except by a reviewer.

Manufactured in the United States of America

CPSIA compliance information: Batch #CW25ENS: For further information contact Enslow Publishing LLC at 1-800-398-2504.

Please visit our website, www.enslowpublishing.com. For a free color catalog of all our high-quality books, call toll free 1-800-398-2504 or fax 1-877-980-4454.

Find us on

Image Credits

All images are courtesy of Shutterstock.com. With thanks to Getty Images, Thinkstock Photo and iStockphoto.
Cover – Rita_Kochmarjova, fotorauschen, Svetsol, ARTvektor. Throughout – Eva Speshneva, ARTvektor, Svetsol, Verock. 2–3 – OlegRi. 4–5 – Kwadrat, Alla-V. 6–7 – from O, Christin Noelle. 8–9 – happylights, Yuriy Mazur. 10–11 – Pixel-Shot, Khamkhor. 12–13 – Nastenok, Bobs Creek Photography. 14–15 – Lenkadan, OlesyaNickolaeva, Vera Zinkova. 16–17 – Puhach Andrei, Rita_Kochmarjova. 18–19 – Justyna Furmanczyk Gibaszek, Sari ONeal. 20–21 – Katrina Leigh, Anastasija Popova. 22–23 – Katrin-ps, Kent Weakley.

Contents

Page 4	Horse
Page 6	Head
Page 8	Eyes
Page 10	Mouth
Page 12	Mane
Page 14	Body
Page 16	Tail
Page 18	Legs
Page 20	Hooves
Page 22	Life Cycle
Page 24	Glossary and Index

Words that look like <u>this</u> can be found in the glossary on page 24.

Horse

Horses are known for their super speed and beautiful hair. Many horses have been <u>domesticated</u>. However, there are still some horses in the wild. These horses can be found near grasslands and woodlands.

The place an animal or plant lives is called its habitat.

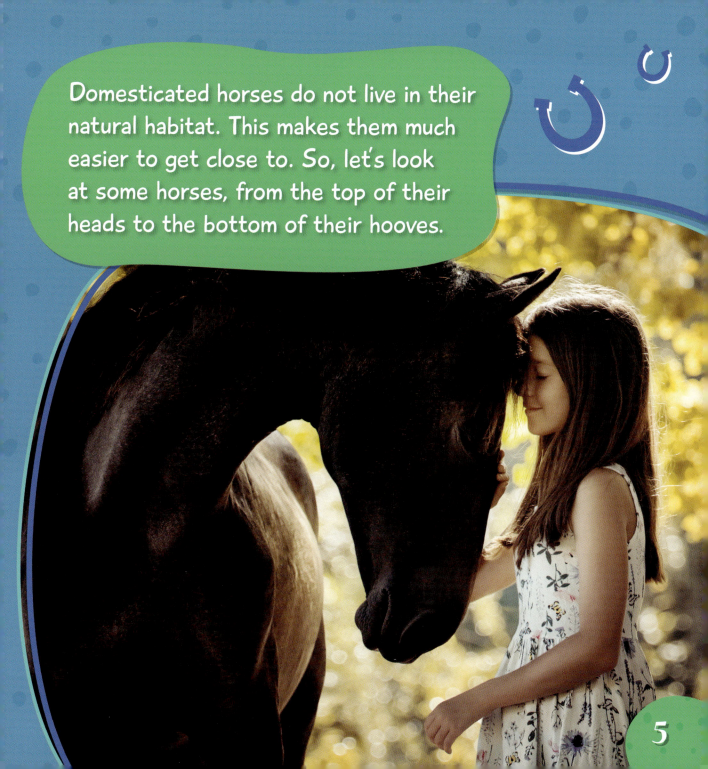

Domesticated horses do not live in their natural habitat. This makes them much easier to get close to. So, let's look at some horses, from the top of their heads to the bottom of their hooves.

Head

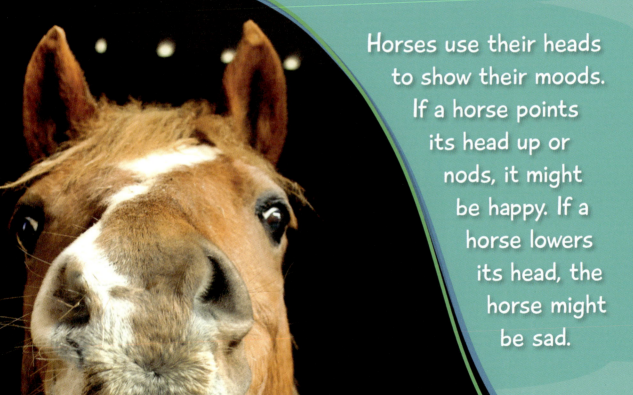

Horses use their heads to show their moods. If a horse points its head up or nods, it might be happy. If a horse lowers its head, the horse might be sad.

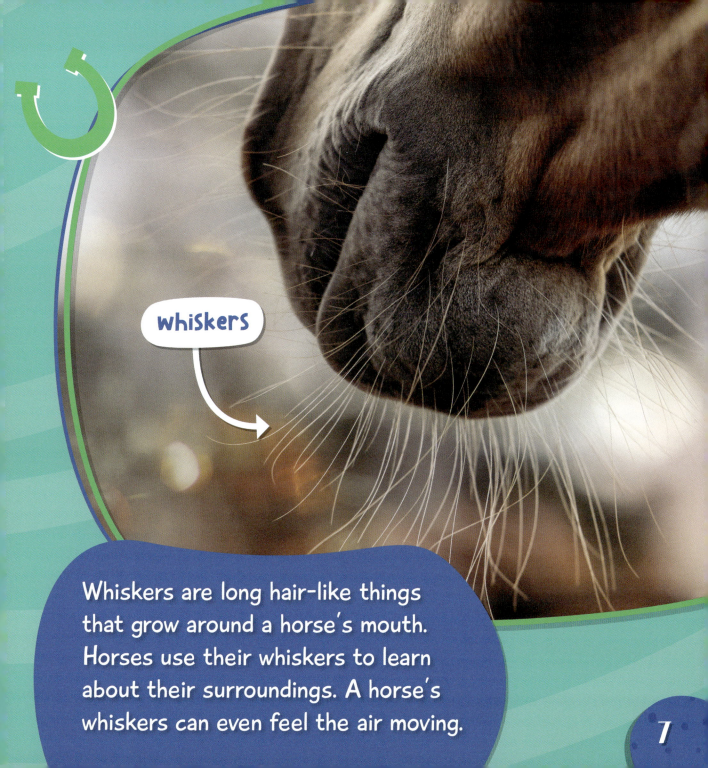

whiskers

Whiskers are long hair-like things that grow around a horse's mouth. Horses use their whiskers to learn about their surroundings. A horse's whiskers can even feel the air moving.

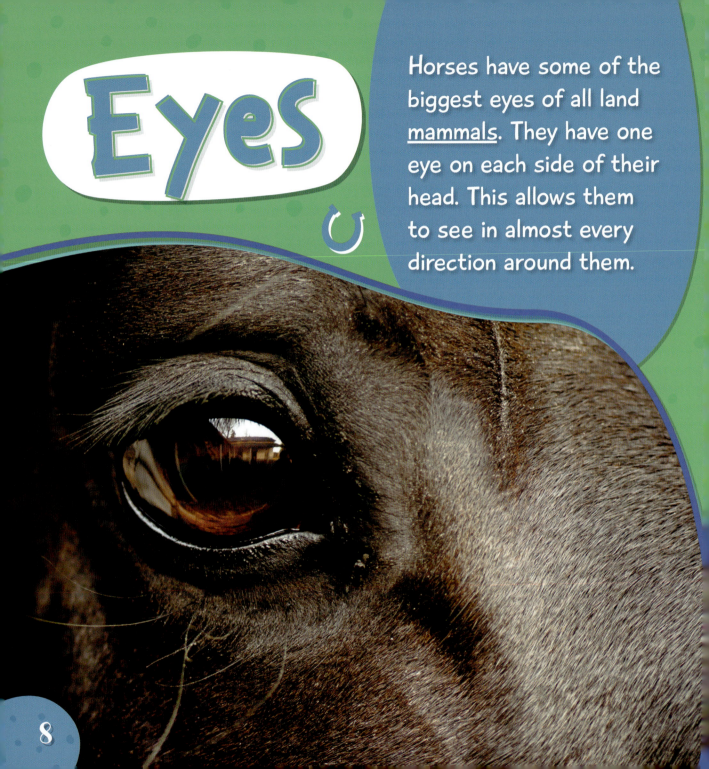

Eyes

Horses have some of the biggest eyes of all land <u>mammals</u>. They have one eye on each side of their head. This allows them to see in almost every direction around them.

Horses can either use both eyes together, like humans do, or they can use each eye on its own. This means they can see two things at once. Horses can also see in the dark.

Mouth

Horses have lots of big teeth. They have between 36 and 40 teeth. Each tooth is around 5 inches (12.7 cm) long. That is longer than an adult person's finger.

Horses cannot breathe through their mouths.

Horses are herbivores, which means they only eat plants. Their teeth are perfect for chewing plants. All horses eat grass. Domestic horses might also be fed hay or vegetables such as carrots.

Horses spend most of the day eating.

Mane

The mane is the hair that starts at the neck and goes down the horse's back. Many horses have thick manes. In the wild, horses use their manes to keep warm in cold habitats.

mane

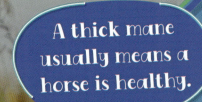

A thick mane usually means a horse is healthy.

12

Some <u>male</u> horses are known as stallions. <u>Female</u> horses are known as mares. Stallions have thicker manes than mares. Stallions need thicker manes to help protect their necks when they fight with other stallions.

Stallions fight to decide the leader of the group.

13

Body

There are hundreds of different types of horses. These different types of horses are called <u>breeds</u>. Different breeds of horses may be different sizes, colors, or have different patterns.

Haflinger horse

Shetland pony

Some horse breeds are taller than others.

14

The hair on a horse's body is called their coat. Horses' coats help to keep their bodies warm in cold weather. Their coats also protect their skin from sunburn.

Clydesdale horse

Tail

Horses' tails are covered by thick hair. Many horses are from cold places, so they need thick hair to keep warm. Their hairy tails protect their hairless behinds from the cold.

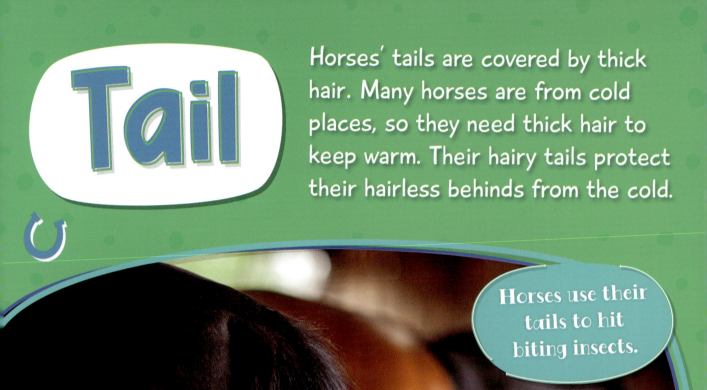

Horses use their tails to hit biting insects.

Legs

Horses have strong legs. Their legs allow them to run fast for a long time. Before cars, people used to ride horses to travel around. It was the fastest way to travel long distances.

Horses' long legs make it difficult to stand up quickly. Therefore, horses can sleep standing up. This allows them to run away from danger even if they have just woken up.

Hooves

Hooves protect the horse's toes. Horses have one <u>solid</u> hoof over each foot. This type of hoof allows horses to run fast and for a long time.

All animals with hooves are called ungulates.

Horses have slightly <u>flexible</u> hooves that can usually protect their feet. People often put metal objects called horseshoes on horse hooves. Horseshoes make the hooves stronger so that people can ride horses without hurting them.

Life Cycle

A baby horse is called a foal. Many mares <u>give birth</u> to foals at night. It is safer for horses to give birth at night because they are less likely to be attacked by <u>predators</u>.

Life cycles are the changes living things go through during their lives, leading up to being able to have their own young.

Horses in the wild can live for 15 to 20 years. Domestic horses live between 25 and 30 years. Domestic horses have lots of food, shelter, and vet care to help them live longer.

Glossary

breeds — groups of animals in the same species that have similar characteristics which set them apart from other animals in the species

domesticated — tamed and kept by humans

female — the sex that can produce offspring or eggs

flexible — having the ability to bend and stretch

give birth — when a mother creates a baby from her body

male — the sex that fathers offspring

mammals — animals that are warm-blooded, have a backbone, and produce milk to feed their children

predators — animals that hunt other animals for food

solid — firm and does not change shape easily

Index

foals 22
hair 4, 7, 12, 15–16
horseshoes 21

mares 13, 22
necks 12–13
plants 4, 11

stallions 13
toes 20
vegetables 11